AF245620

MEMORIES

MEMORIES

Robert Creeley

PIG PRESS
DURHAM
1984

Acknowledgements:
Thanks to **Columbia Magazine**, **Conjunctions** and **The St Marks Poetry Project Newsletter** where some of these poems first appeared.

R.C.

The quotation from "The Mind is an Enchanting Thing" by Marianne Moore is reproduced from her **Collected Works** (copyright 1951) with permission from Macmillan Publishing Co., Inc.

Published by Ric and Ann Caddel at the
Pig Press
7 Cross View Terrace
Neville's Cross
Durham DH1 4JY

Printed at the Arc and Throstle Press, Todmorden

British Library Cataloguing in Publication Data

Creeley, Robert
  Memories.
  I. Title
  811'.54   PS3505.R43

  ISBN 0-903997-82-7
  ISBN 0-903997-83-5 Signed ed.

It has memory's ear
        that can hear without
having to hear.

— from Marianne Moore's
"The Mind is an Enchanting Thing"

CONTENTS

HEAVEN KNOWS

Seemingly never until one's dead
is there possible measure—

but of what then or for what
other than the same plagues

attended the living with misunderstanding
and wanted a compromise as pledge

one could care for any of them
heaven knows, if that's where one goes.

NEW ENGLAND

Work, Christian, work!
Love's labors before you go
carrying lights like the
stars are all out and
tonight is the night.

FORTY

The forthright, good-natured faith
of man hung on crane up

forty stories with roof scaffolding
burning below him forty feet,

good warm face, black hair,
confidence.   He said, when

the fireman appeared, he said
I'm glad to see you,

glad not to be there alone.
How old?   Thirty, thirty-five?

He has friends to believe in,
those who love him.

OUT

Within pitiless
indifference
things left
out.

TOO LATE

You tried to answer the questions attractively,
your name, your particular interests,

what you hoped life would prove,
what you owned and had with you,

your so-called billfold an umbilical,
useless, to the sack you'd carried

all your sad life, all your vulnerability,
but couldn't hide, couldn't now say,

brown hair, brown eyes, steady,
I think I love you.

ROOM

Quick stutters of incidental
passage going back

and forth, quick
breaks of pattern, slices

of the meat, two
rotten tomatoes, an incidental

snowstorm, death, a girl
that looks like you later

than these leaves of
grass, trees, birds, under

water, empty passage-
way, and no way back.

HOTEL

It isn't in the world of
fragile relationships

or memories, nothing
you could have brought with you.

It's snowing in Toronto.
It's four-thirty, a winter evening,

and the tv looks like a faded
hailstorm.   The people

you know are down the hall,
maybe, but you're tired,

you're alone, and that's happy.
Give up and lie down.

ECHO

Pushing out from
this insistent

time makes
all of it

empty, again
memory.

EARTH

And as the world is flat or round
out over those difficult dispositions

of actual water, actual earth,
each thing invariable, specific,

I think no rock's hardness,
call on none to gainsay me,

be only here as and forever
each and every thing is.

DOGS

I've trained them
to come,

to go away again,
to sit, to stand,

to wait
on command,

or I'd like to
be the master who

tells them all
they can't do.

VISION

Think of the size of it,
so big, if you could remember
what it was or where.

RELIGION

Gods one would have
hauled out like props
to shore up the invented
inside-out proposals

of worlds equally like shams
back of a shabby curtain
only let in the duped,
the dumbly despairing.

So flutter the dead
back of the scene
and along with them
the possibly still living.

THE ROCK

Shaking hands again
from place of age,
out to the one

is walking down
the garden path
to be as all reunited.

THANKSGIVING'S DONE

All leaves gone, yellow
light with low sun,

branches edged
in sharpened outline

against far up pale sky.
Nights with their blackness

and myriad stars, colder
now as these days go by.

MOTHER'S THINGS

I wanted approval,
carrying with me
things of my mother's
beyond their use to me—

worn-out clock,
her small green lock box,
father's engraved brass plate
for printing calling cards—

such size of her still
calls out to me
with that silently
expressive will.

ECHO

Lonely in
no one
to hold it with—

the responsible
caring
for those one's known.

FOR PEN

Lady moon
light white
flowers open
in sweet silence.

FOR J.D.

Seeing is believing—
times such things
alter all one
had known.

These times, places,
old, echoing
clothes, hands—tools,
almost walking.

Your heart *as big as all outdoors...*
where tree grows,
gate was
waiting.

ALWAYS

Sweet sister Mary's gone
away.   Time fades on and on.

The morning was so bright, so clear
blurs in the eye, fades also.

Time tells what after all.
It's always now, always here.

EDGE

Edge of place
put on between

its proposed
place in

time
and space.

MASSACHUSETTS MAY

Month one was born in
particular emphasis
as year comes round
again.   Laconic, diverse

sweet May of my boyhood,
as the Memorial Day Parade
marches through those memories.
Or else the hum and laze

of summer's sweet patterns,
dragonflies, grasshoppers,
ladyslippers, and ponds—
School's end.   Summer's song.

MEMORIES

Hello, duck,
in yellow

cloth stuffed from
inside out,

little
pillow.

ECHO

Back in time
for supper
when the lights